MOTORMANIA

CLASSIC CARS

ROB COLSON

CRABTREE
PUBLISHING COMPANY
WWW.CRABTREEBOOKS.COM

CRABTREE
PUBLISHING COMPANY
WWW.CRABTREEBOOKS.COM

Author: Rob Colson
Editorial director: Kathy Middleton
Series editor: John Hort
Editor: Crystal Sikkens
Designer: Jonathan Vipond
Proofreader: Wendy Scavuzzo
Production technician: Margaret Salter
Print coordinator: Katherine Berti

Picture Credits
t-top, b-bottom, l-left, r-right, c-center, front cover-fc,
back cover-bc
fc Hakan Akdemir / Shutterstock.com, bc Martin Charles Hatch/ Shutterstock.com,
1, 20-21t, 20-21c, 20b, 21c Alexander Kirch/ Shutterstock.com, 7t, 17c, 17b BMW, 6b
Vividrange/ Shutterstock.com, 4 Alberto Zamorano / Shutterstock.com, 5tr
DeFacto/CC, 5c PRESSLAB / Shutterstock.com, 5b Nejron Photo / Shutterstock.com,
6-7 J HIME / Shutterstock.com, 7t SunflowerMomma / Shutterstock.com, 7b Tony
Craddock / Shutterstock.com, 8-9 Alf van Beem, 9t Mr.choppers/CC, 9b Brody
Levesque/CC, 10l Bundesarchiv, 10-11, 11tr Hakan Akdemir / Shutterstock.com, 11tc
Bukk, 11b Morio/CC, 12-13t Gaschwald / Shutterstock.com, 12-13b Mike van
Schoonderwalt / Shutterstock.com, 13tr Corepics VOF / Shutterstock.com, 13b
Grzegorz Czapski / Shutterstock.com, 14-15t, 14-15c, 14-15b Keith Bell /
Shutterstock.com, 15t EB Adventure Photography / Shutterstock.com, 15b Bene
Riobó/CC, 16-17 Martin Charles Hatch / Shutterstock.com, 18-19, 19t, 19c Jaguar
Land Rover Limited, 18b, 19b Rudiecast / Shutterstock.com, 21t OleksSH /
Shutterstock.com, 21b Roman Belogorodov / Shutterstock.com, 22-23 Sergey Kohl
/ Shutterstock.com, 22bl Agia / Shutterstock.com, 22br David MG/ Shutterstock.
com, 23c Ed Aldridge / Shutterstock.com, 22b Steve Lagreca / Shutterstock.com,
24-25, 24b, 25t, 25b, 32 Toyota, 26-27 ermess / Shutterstock.com, 26b D-VISIONS /
Shutterstock.com, 27t J HIME / Shutterstock.com, 27bl Giannis Papanikos /
Shutterstock.com, 27br Gaschwald / Shutterstock.com, 28 Roman Belogorodov /
Shutterstock.com, 28-29t BMW, 28-29b Suat Eracar / Shutterstock.com
Every attempt has been made to clear copyright. Should
there be any inadvertent omission, please apply to the
publisher for rectification.

First published in Great Britain
in 2020 by Wayland
Copyright © Hodder and Stoughton, 2020
All rights reserved

Library and Archives Canada Cataloguing in Publication

CIP Available at the Library and Archives Canada

Library of Congress Cataloging-in-Publication Data

CIP Available at the Library of Congress

Crabtree Publishing Company
www.crabtreebooks.com   1-800-387-7650

Published by Crabtree Publishing Company in 2022.

Printed in the U.S.A./012022/CG20210915

Published in Canada
Crabtree Publishing
616 Welland Ave.
St. Catharines, Ontario
L2M 5V6

Published in the United States
Crabtree Publishing
347 Fifth Ave
Suite 1402-145
New York, NY 10016

CONTENTS

WHAT IS A CLASSIC CAR?

Classic cars are old models that people enjoy owning, restoring, and collecting. Some are very rare and can be sold for a lot of money. Owners of classic cars take great care of their vehicles to keep them in their original condition.

Many classic car owners bring their vehicles out each year at the Rally of Vintage Cars in Barcelona, Spain, which is exclusively for cars made before 1925.

CLASSIC OR VINTAGE?

Any car model that is no longer made may be called a classic if enough people still want to own it. However, most classic cars are at least 40 years old. Cars made before the 1940s are also called vintage cars. These very old cars need a lot of maintenance to keep them in working order.

Vintage Volkswagen Beetles at a rally in New York

MOVIE STARS

Some cars achieve classic status with the help of movie appearances. British sports car manufacturer Aston Martin has provided a car for 12 different James Bond movies. Their first appearance came in the 1964 film *Goldfinger*. Aston Martin made two models of the DB5 for the film, one of which was fitted with gadgets for Bond to use.

CLASSIC RESTORATION

Old cars in poor condition can be bought for cheap and restored. For many owners, working on an old wreck is a labor of love. The engines may need to be rebuilt, replacing worn-out components. Restoring the bodywork can take hundreds of hours of work. Dents must be hammered out, while some panels may need replacing. The whole thing needs to be repainted at the end.

ROLLS-ROYCE
SILVER GHOST

First made in 1907, the Silver Ghost is the car that established British company Rolls-Royce as the leading luxury car manufacturer. It was described at the time as "the best car in the world."

SPIRIT OF ECSTASY

At the front of the hood of Rolls-Royce cars sits the Spirit of Ecstasy emblem. It takes the form of a woman leaning forward with her arms outstretched as if she had wings. Designed by sculptor Charles Sykes, it has been featured on every Rolls-Royce car since 1911.

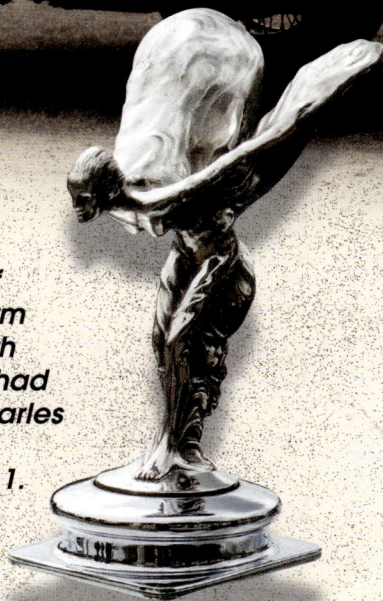

TECH POINT

In 1907, Rolls-Royce demonstrated the reliability of their new model by driving it between London and Glasgow 27 times— a distance of 14,371 miles (23,128 km). Engineers checked the car at the end of the test and found that the engine was still in good working order.

SILVER GHOST

YEARS OF PRODUCTION:
1907–1926

NUMBER BUILT:
7,874 (nearly 1,500 still survive)

ENGINE:
7 liter, 6 cylinders

POWER:
48 **horsepower (hp)**

TOP SPEED:
63 mph (100 kph)

TODAY'S VALUE:
Up to $41 million

*The engine contained six large **cylinders** in one line.*

QUIET RUNNING

Rolls-Royce originally called the car the 40/50 hp, after its power capabilities. However, this name proved to be too dull. Journalists soon nicknamed it the "Silver Ghost" after the color of the first model and the smooth, quiet running of its engine.

The folding roof was made of black canvas.

PRIZED POSSESSION
Surviving models of the Silver Ghost are some of the most valuable cars in the world. The car that was tested in 1907 is still in working order more than a century later, and is thought to be worth more than US $41 million.

LINCOLN
K SERIES

Low sloping windshield

The K Series was a line of luxury cars produced by American manufacturer Lincoln. These elegant cars were popular among Hollywood stars in the 1930s.

K SERIES

YEARS OF PRODUCTION:
1931–1940

ENGINE:
6.3 liter, 8 cylinders, or 7.3 liter, 12 cylinders

POWER:
150 hp (V12 model)

TOP SPEED:
90 mph (145 kph) (V12 model)

TODAY'S VALUE:
$55,000 – $69,000
depending on the model

CHOICE OF THE WEALTHY

The K Series came in many different styles and options, allowing Lincoln's wealthy clients to customize their vehicles. Many were designed to be driven by a **chauffeur**, with a driver's compartment that was separated from the rest of the car.

TECH POINT

Cars in the 1930s had narrow bodies that sat high off the ground. They were fitted with running boards to help people to climb in and out. Lincoln made their running boards into a stylish feature, sweeping back from the front fenders. The boards could also be used to carry luggage or even pets!

A detachable rack could be placed above the small trunk to provide extra space for luggage.

Running board

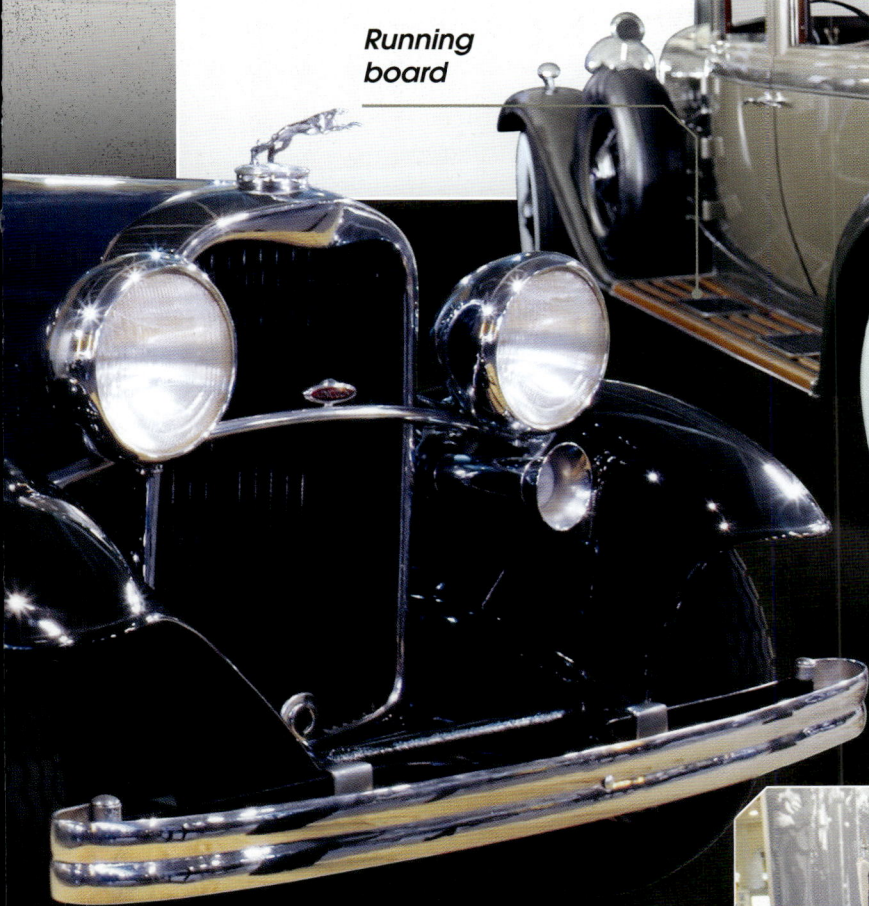

Wide fenders were attached to the running boards.

SUNSHINE SPECIAL

In 1939, Lincoln built a special edition of the K Series for US President Franklin D. Roosevelt to use as his official state car. It was nicknamed the "Sunshine Special" after its retractable roof, which Roosevelt liked to keep open during public appearances.

VOLKSWAGEN BEETLE

With more than 21 million built in nearly 70 years of production, the Volkswagen Beetle was the most popular car ever made. Its overall shape remained almost unchanged over the decades, but the engine and other mechanical systems were updated as technology improved.

FERDINAND PORSCHE

The Beetle was designed by Austrian engineer Ferdinand Porsche (1875–1951), founder of the Porsche sports car company. Porsche placed the engine at the rear and created an **aerodynamic** shape for the Beetle. Today, Porsche is a divisive figure in Germany due to his close association with the Nazis.

THE PEOPLE'S CAR

The word Volkswagen means "people's car." The Beetle was commissioned by the Nazi German Chancellor Adolf Hitler, who wanted a cheap reliable car that could carry a family of four and maintain a speed of 62 mph (100 kph) on Germany's new motorways. It was first made in 1938, but mass production did not start until 1946, after World War II (1939–1945).

Bumpers wear out and need to be replaced every few years. They can still be bought from specialist suppliers.

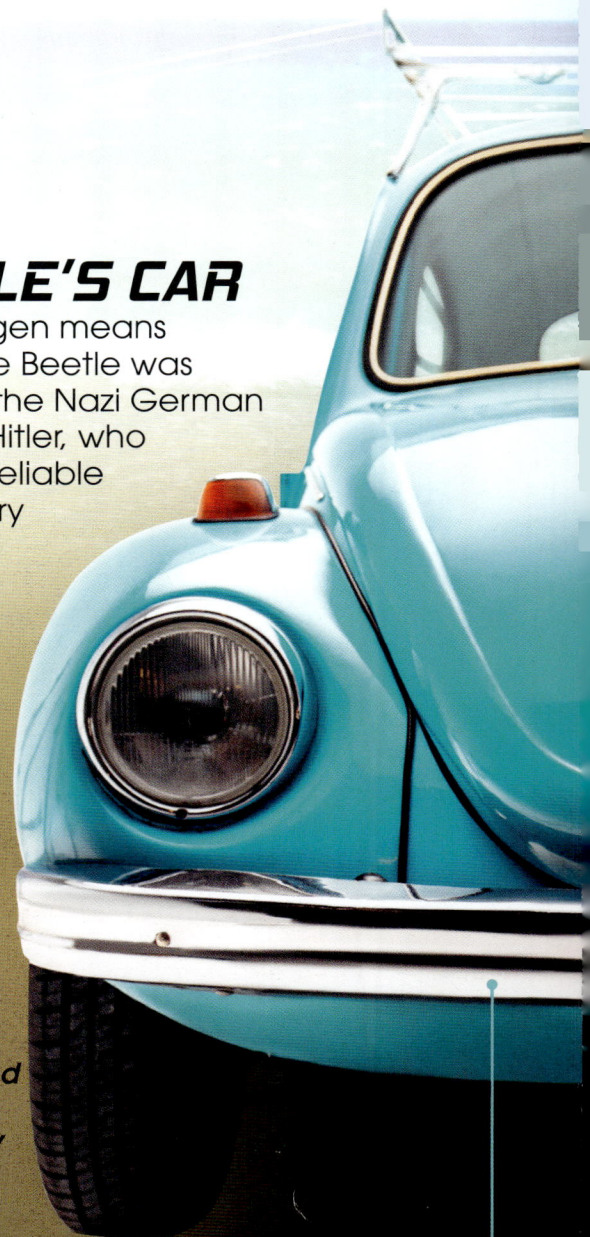

AIR-COOLED

The Beetle was one of the first mass-produced cars to have its engine at the back. That allowed more space for passengers, but it increased the danger that the engine would overheat. To avoid that, air was directed down from the top of the car to keep the engine cool.

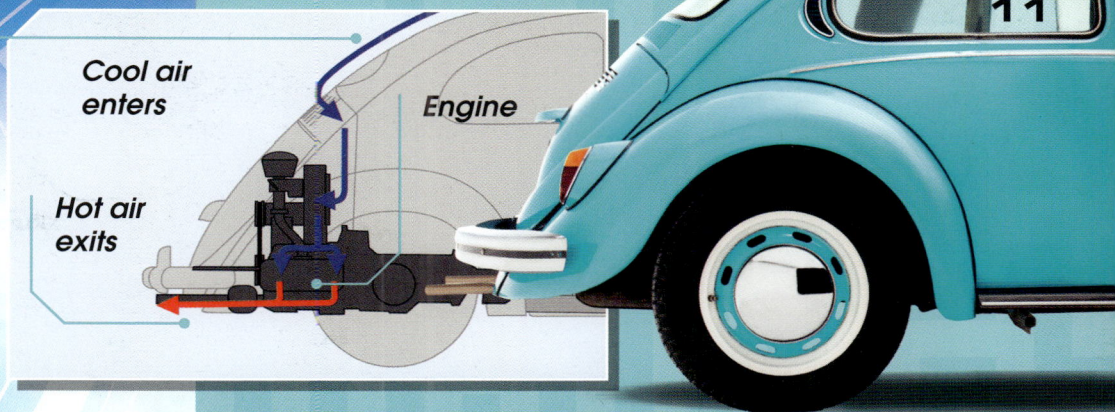

Cool air enters

Hot air exits

Engine

BEETLE

YEARS OF PRODUCTION:
1938–2003

NUMBER BUILT:
21,529,464

ENGINE:
1.1 liter, 4 cylinders (1938)

POWER:
25 hp

TOP SPEED:
62 mph (100 kph)
(1938 model)

TODAY'S VALUE:
An original Type 1 in good condition is worth more than $13,000, with rare models reaching far more.

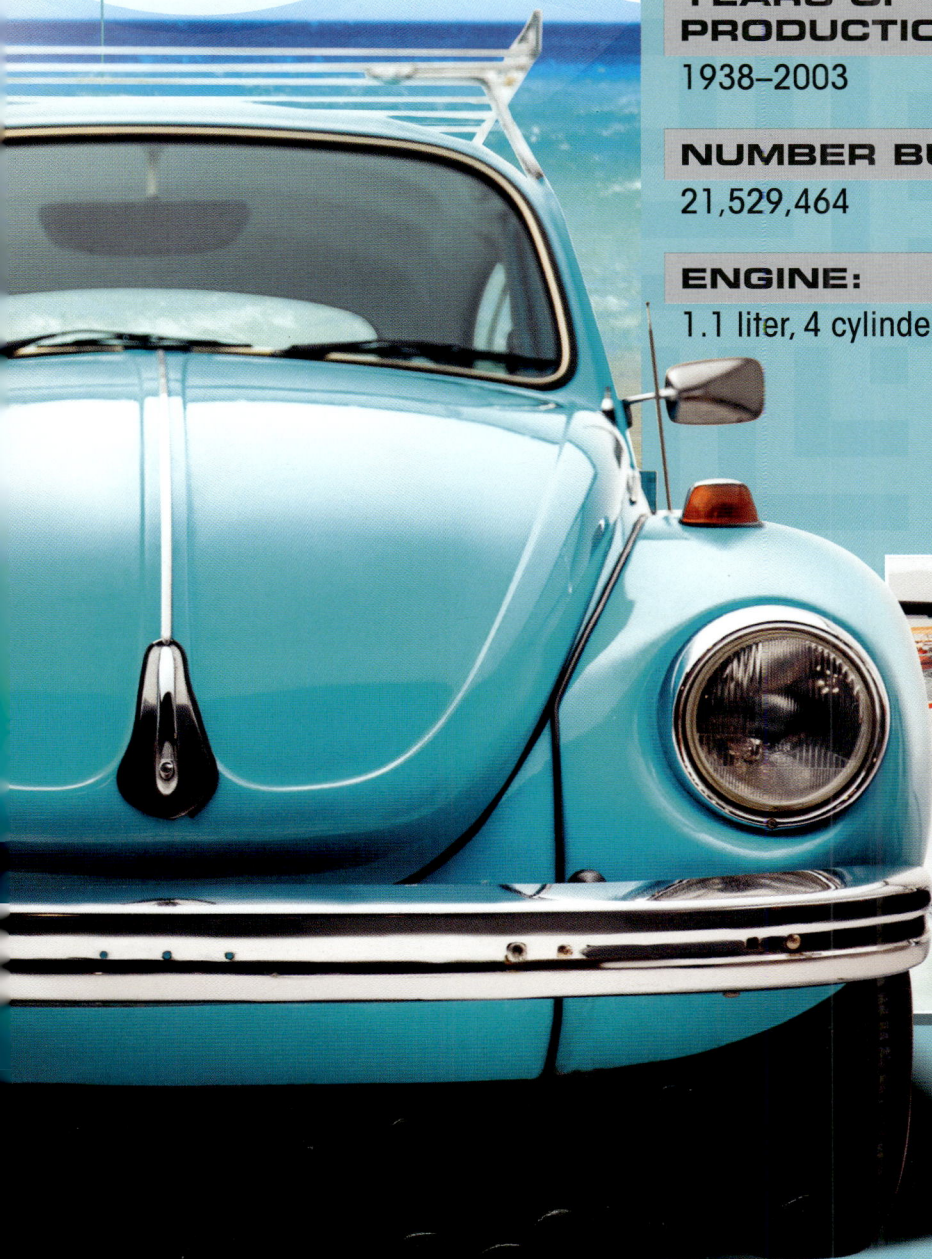

Early models of the Type 1 Beetle, such as this one from 1950, had distinctive split rear windows. Today, models with this feature are highly sought-after.

CITROËN
DS

First made in 1955, the Citroën DS was a mid-size luxury car packed with the latest technology. In French, its name sounds like the word "déesse," meaning goddess, and it soon became a symbol of French innovation and style.

ANDRÉ LEFÈBVRE

Three of Citroën's most successful cars were created by André Lefèbvre (1894–1964). In addition to the DS, he designed the Traction Avant, the first front-wheel-drive production car, and the 2CV, a small car introduced in 1948 to compete with the VW Beetle. Before joining Citroën, Lefèbvre had a successful career as a racecar driver.

HIGH-TECH SUSPENSION
To deal with France's bumpy roads, the DS was built with a self-leveling *suspension* operated by *hydraulics*. The suspension could adjust itself on each wheel independently to keep the car level.

The suspension gave passengers the feeling that the car was floating, which was compared to riding on a magic carpet.

On the 1967 DS, headlights rotated to point in the same direction as the front wheels.

NEW IDEAS

In addition to its innovative suspension system, the DS was the first production car to feature **disc brakes**. It was also fitted with a hydraulically controlled **gearbox**, meaning that there was no need for a **clutch** pedal. The wheels at the front were wider apart than those at the back, which improved the **handling**.

DS

YEARS OF PRODUCTION:
1955–1975

ENGINE:
1.9–2.3 liter, 4 cylinders

POWER:
75 hp (1955 model)
141 hp (1972 model)

TOP SPEED:
90 mph (145 kph)

TODAY'S VALUE:
from $41,000

When the engine was turned on, the hydraulics raised the whole car up.

PLYMOUTH
FURY

The Plymouth Fury has become a symbol of 1950s America. Big, heavy, and with an engine that guzzled gas, this full-size car was made at a time when fuel was cheap and style was important.

Curved windows resemble those of a jet plane's cockpit.

FURY

YEARS OF PRODUCTION:
1955–1960 (original version)

ENGINE:
5–5.9 liter, 8 cylinders

POWER:
up to 305 hp

TOP SPEED:
124 mph (200 kph)

TODAY'S VALUE:
up to $69,000

Huge chrome-plated front bumper and grille

SPACE-AGE STYLE

Like many American cars in the 1950s, the Fury was fitted with two large tailfins. They were shaped to resemble the engine sections of jet fighters or space rockets. Plymouth claimed the tailfins helped to keep the car stable in crosswinds but, in reality, they were all about looks. Tailfins went out of style in the 1960s amid safety concerns about sharp parts on cars.

Chrome-plated trim pieces

Tailfin

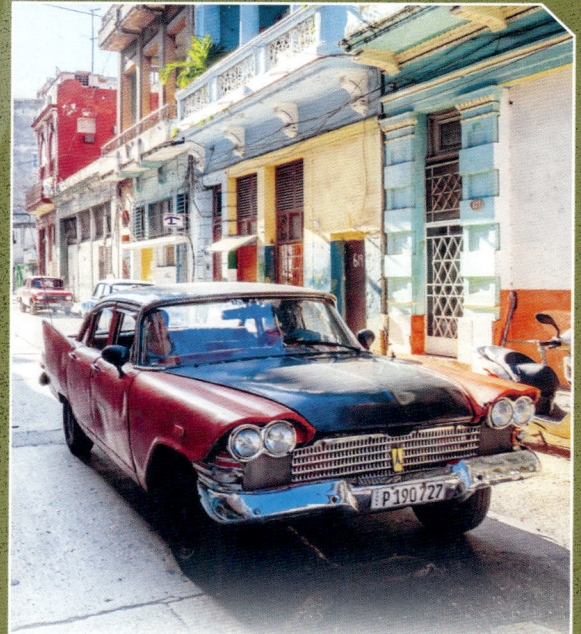

CUBAN CLASSICS

Many classic 1950s American cars are still running on the roads in Cuba. Thousands of people immigrated to the United States after the Cuban Revolution in 1959, but they had to leave their American cars behind. Over time, the original parts have often been replaced with parts from other cars, such as engines from a Lada, which is a small car made in the Soviet Union (now called Russia).

STATION WAGON

An even bigger version of the Fury was available in the form of a station wagon. These are cars with an extended back end to provide more cargo space. Today, they have largely been replaced by sport utility vehicles (SUVs).

BMC
MINI

The best-selling British car of all time, the Mini, was a small car famed for its space and handling. Designed to be basic and affordable, the Mini became a style icon in the 1960s and the original Mark 1 model is now a highly desirable collector's item.

FUEL CRISIS

In the late 1950s, Britain was experiencing an oil crisis and fuel was rationed. Sales of large cars collapsed, while small cars from Germany and Italy became very popular because they used less fuel. The Mini was the British Motor Corporation's response to the crisis. It was economical, but still had space for four adults and gave a sharp, responsive drive, despite its small engine.

MINI

YEARS OF PRODUCTION:
1959–2000

ENGINE:
1.1 liter, 4 cylinders
(Mark 1)

SINGLE STRUCTURE

The Mini had a single **monocoque** body, a cutting-edge technology at the time that saved space.

The wheels were just 10 inches (25 cm) in diameter. That saved even more space.

Alec Issigonis' hand-drawn sketch shows his idea for a sideways-mounted engine.

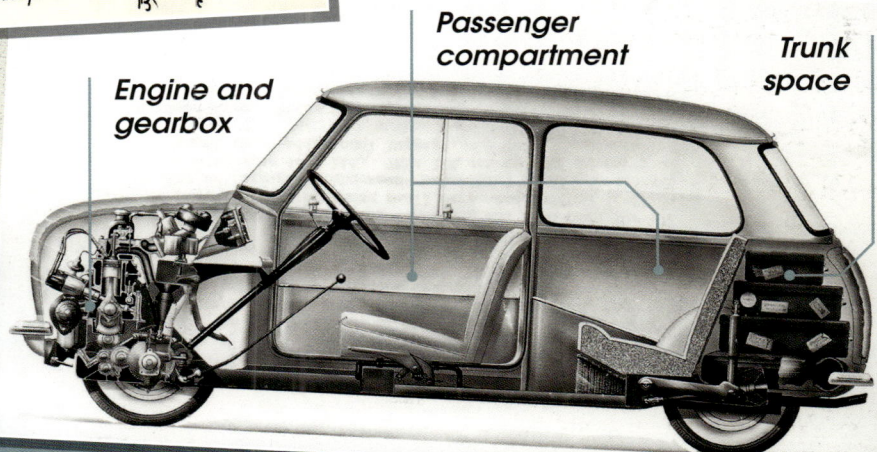

ALEC ISSIGONIS

Designer Alec Issigonis (1906–1988) created the shape of the Mini and was also responsible for developing its space-saving innovations. The guiding idea behind his designs was that people who drive small cars are the same size as those who drive large cars, and the cars need to reflect that.

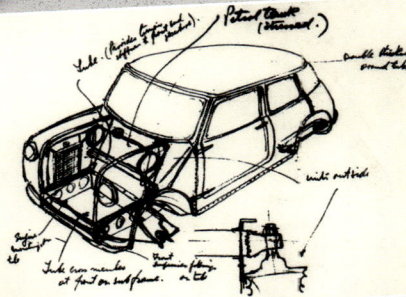

Engine and gearbox

Passenger compartment

Trunk space

POWER:
70 hp

TOP SPEED:
93 mph (150 kph)

TODAY'S VALUE:
1960s cars sell for $14,000 or more

MAXIMUM SPACE

Eighty percent of the Mini's area was used by passengers and luggage. To achieve this, the engine sat sideways at the front and the car was front-wheel drive. The suspension saved space by using rubber cones instead of springs. That made for a bumpy ride, but also gave excellent handling.

JAGUAR
E-TYPE

The E-Type is a two-seater sports car that combines high performance with style. The car was described by Enzo Ferrari, founder of the Ferrari motor racing team, as "the most beautiful car ever made."

Hard-top coupé

E-TYPE

YEARS OF PRODUCTION:
1961–1975

ENGINE:
3.8–4.2 liter, 6 cylinders (Series 1)

POWER:
265 hp

DASH TO GENEVA

The E-Type was first shown to the public at the 1961 Geneva Motor Show. Jaguar only took the coupé version, but it proved such a hit that they wanted to show off the open-top roadster (left), too. Test driver Norman Dewis jumped in the roadster version at the Jaguar factory in Coventry, England, and drove through the night to reach Geneva in 11 hours, covering a distance of 621 miles (1,000 km).

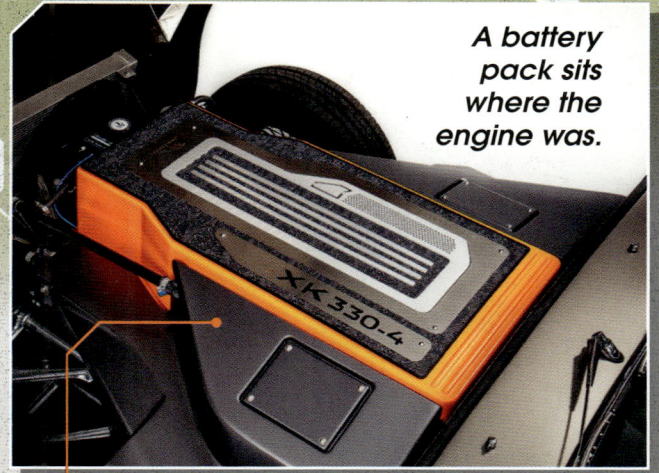

A battery pack sits where the engine was.

MODERN TAKE

In 2018, Jaguar produced the E-Type Zero, replacing the E-Type's gas engine with an electric motor. The motor and battery were the same size and weight as the original engine so that the car kept its perfect balance.

TECH POINT

The E-Type's distinctive long hood and sleek curves were created by Malcolm Sayer (1916–1970). An aircraft engineer during World War II, Sayer knew how important aerodynamics was to high-speed performance. In the days before computer design, he used mathematical formulas to create the car's curves. He attached absorbent cotton to the hood during testing to see how air flowed over it.

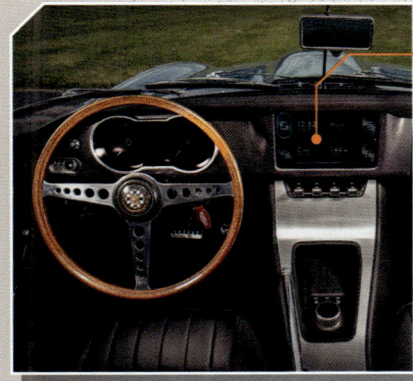

The display on the dashboard of the E-Type Zero shows how much battery power is left.

TOP SPEED:
149 mph (240 kph)

0-60 MPH (97 KPH):
7 seconds

TODAY'S VALUE:
from **$137,600**

PORSCHE
911

The 911 was designed by Butzi Porsche, grandson of the creator of the VW Beetle (see page 10). With more than 1 million cars made and sold, the 911 has been in production since 1963, undergoing continuous improvements while its basic shape has remained the same.

911

Like the VW Beetle, the 911's engine is at the back.

YEARS OF PRODUCTION:
1963–1989

ENGINE:
2–3.3 liter, 6 cylinder

POWER:
130 hp (1963)

TODAY'S VALUE:
From $28,000 up to $1.4 million for a Carrera RS 2.7

RACING SUCCESS

As well as being a road car, the original 911 series produced from 1963 to 1989, was one of the most successful racecars in history, winning titles both on the track and in off-road rallies. A heavily modified 911, known as the 935, won the prestigious 24 Hours of Le Mans **endurance race** in 1979.

*The 935 that won at Le Mans had a long tail and a huge rear wing to produce maximum **downforce**. It was nicknamed "Moby Dick."*

The trunk is at the front, under the hood.

TECH POINT

In 1966, Porsche improved the performance of the 911 by fitting its sports model with new lightweight wheels called Fuchs wheels. Made from a light aluminum **alloy**, the wheels were forged in one piece using a process invented by metal specialist Otto Fuchs. The weight saved gave the car a crucial advantage in track races.

PRIZED MODEL

While all original 911s are classic cars, some are much more valuable than others. One of the rarest and most sought-after is the 1973 Carrera RS 2.7. This model was stripped of all non-essential parts to produce a lightweight racecar that generated 210 hp.

FORD
MUSTANG

MUSTANG

YEARS OF PRODUCTION:
1965–1973 (first generation)

ENGINE:
2.8–7.0 liter, 6–8 cylinders

POWER:
375 hp (7 liter engine)

TOP SPEED:
118 mph (190 kph)

0–60 MPH (97 KPH):
7 seconds

TODAY'S VALUE:
From $28,000

Ford created a new kind of car with the Mustang. It was a powerful car with a large engine housed under a long hood, a style that became known as a "pony car." Many rival American manufacturers produced similar models over the next few years, but the Mustang is the original and, for many, the best.

Coupé version

Convertible version

The "fastback" version of the Mustang had a sloping rear window and trunk.

INSTANT HIT

The first generation of the Mustang was produced from 1965 to 1973. It proved an instant hit in the United States, with more than 1 million sold in the first 18 months of production. The car was revised several times, making it bigger and more powerful. It was replaced by the smaller, more economical Mustang II in 1974, following a rise in the price of gas.

CLASSIC CHASE

The Mustang achieved worldwide fame in 1968 when it was featured in the film Bullitt. Pursued by a Dodge Charger, it was involved in one of the longest car chases in film history. The chase lasted more than ten minutes on screen, and took three weeks to film.

TECH POINT

To develop their ideas for a pony car, Ford made two **concept cars**. The Mustang I, made in 1962, was a mid-engined car with a streamlined hood. Ford worried that it would be hard to make, so they created a front-engine version, the Mustang II, a year later. The Mustang II was a hit at car shows, and the car went into production shortly afterward.

Mustang 1 concept car

TOYOTA
2000GT

This limited-edition sports car changed the world's perception of Japanese cars. Japan was known for vehicles that were more practical than stylish. The 2000GT was the exact opposite: beautiful but cramped.

The car was just 3.8 feet (1.2 m) high.

Two narrow chrome bumpers protected the front and back of the car.

RARE MODEL

Just 351 2000GTs were built, and it is widely thought of today as Japan's first **supercar**. Toyota treated it as a "halo car," meaning it lost them money but gave the company great publicity. Today, its rarity makes it extremely valuable, and one fully restored model sold in 2013 for $1.2 million.

BOND CAR

A unique open-top roadster version of the 2000GT was built for the 1967 Bond movie *You Only Live Twice*. The roof had to be removed because the actor playing James Bond, Sean Connery, was too tall to fit inside.

2000 GT

YEARS OF PRODUCTION:
1967–1970

ENGINE:
2.0–2.3 liter, 6 cylinder

POWER:
150 hp

TOP SPEED:
130 mph (209 kph)

0–60 MPH (97 KPH):
10 seconds

TODAY'S VALUE:
Up to $1.2 million

The wheels were fitted with power-assisted disc brakes.

TECH POINT

Toyota designer Satoru Nozaki was influenced by the Jaguar E-Type (see page 18) in his design for the 2000GT. He took the E-Type's basic shape and made it even more aerodynamic by shortening and narrowing it. He also lowered the nose and hood, which meant the car had to be fitted with pop-up headlights to comply with the minimum height requirements in California, an important market for sports cars.

Pop-up headlights

246 GT

In 1969, Ferrari joined forces with fellow Italian carmaker Fiat to produce the Dino, a series of relatively affordable sports cars to rival Porsche's 911 (see page 20). Today, the Dino 246 GT is worth far more than its original selling price.

The Dino 246 GT had softer, more rounded edges than a typical Ferrari.

NEW MARQUE

The Dino marque is named after the son of Enzo Ferrari, the company's founder. Alfredo "Dino" Ferrari died in 1956, at just 24 years of age. At the time, he had been working on a small V6 engine for Formula 2 racing. His engine was used for the first Dino, the 206 GT.

TECH POINT

Ferrari used the Dino engine from the late 1950s to the early 2000s. In the Ferrari Dino cars, the engine was placed sideways mid-car. That left little room for the driver and passenger, but gave the car excellent balance and allowed for a streamlined hood.

246 GT

YEARS OF PRODUCTION:
1969–1974

ENGINE:
2.4 liter, 6 cylinders

POWER:
190 hp

TOP SPEED:
146 mph (235 kph)

TODAY'S VALUE:
$400,000

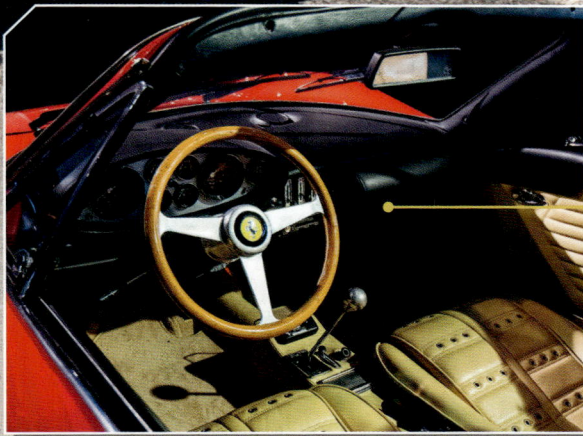

The interior was cramped, so there was no room for a glove compartment on the passenger side.

FIAT DINO
Fiat built the engine for the Ferrari Dino, and used it to make a Dino range of their own. They moved the engine to the front to allow more room inside. The Fiat Dino has also become a classic, and today it is worth up to $138,000.

BMW

E9

BMW's E9 was a range of high-performance two-door coupés. It was highly successful in touring car races, and helped to establish the German manufacturer's reputation for well-built, sporty, luxury cars.

Hofmeister kink

E9

DISTINCTIVE KINK

BMW cars have several distinctive design features that make them instantly recognizable. One of these is the "Hofmeister kink," a curve in the back corner of the rear window. It was first introduced in 1961 by head of design Wilhelm Hofmeister, who was also in charge of the design of the E9. The kink has featured on nearly all BMW cars ever since.

YEARS OF PRODUCTION:
1968–1975

ENGINE:
2.5–3.2 liter, 6 cylinders

POWER:
203 hp (CSL)

The 3.0 CLS was fitted with a rear wing for racing.

TECH POINT

In 1972, BMW produced a special racing version of the E9 called the 3.0 CSL. The car was made as light as possible by stripping out the soundproofing, and using thinner steel for the body, aluminum for the doors, hood, and trunk, and plexiglass for the side windows. Just 1,265 cars were built, and today the CSL is a rare collector's item.

TOP SPEED:
133 mph (214 kph) (CSL)

TODAY'S VALUE:
$250,000 (CSL)

ART CAR
BMW has a tradition of asking famous artists to create unique paint jobs for their cars. The first of these "Art Cars" was an E9 3.0 CSL painted by American artist Alexander Calder. He chose the bright colors his artwork was known for. The car was raced at the 1975 24 Hours of Le Mans.

GLOSSARY

aerodynamic
Made in a way that allows a gas or liquid to move around it smoothly. Engineers study aerodynamics to produce cars with a shape that allows air to move around them smoothly.

alloy
A material made by mixing two or more metals or by mixing metal with other substances

chauffeur
A professional driver employed to drive a private car

clutch
A mechanism in a car, normally operated by a pedal, that disconnects the engine from the gearbox to allow the driver to change gears

concept car
An experimental model made by car manufacturers to test out new ideas

coupé
A car with a fixed roof and two doors

cylinders
The parts of an engine inside which fuel burns to pump pistons and generate power

disc brakes
Brakes that slow a car down by clamping a pair of pads against a disc that is attached to each wheel

downforce
A force that pushes down on a car to keep it on the road. Parts of a racecar are designed to generate the right amount of downforce without slowing the car down too much.

endurance race
A race in which cars drive as far as they can within a fixed amount of time

gearbox
The system of gears in a car. Gears change the speed at which the engine's power drives the wheels.

handling
The ease with which a driver can control a car

horsepower (hp)
A unit of measurement for power, or the rate at which work is done. One horsepower is roughly equal to the power of one strong horse.

hydraulics
A power system in which fluids are used to transfer force from one place to another

monocoque
A strong exterior shell of a vehicle that provides it with structural support

supercar
A sports car that is very powerful, very fast, and very expensive

suspension
A system of springs and shock absorbers that attach the wheels to a car's chassis

FACT FILE

RARE CLASSIC CARS SOMETIMES COME UP AT PUBLIC AUCTIONS. HERE ARE SOME OF THE HIGHEST PRICES THEY HAVE REACHED.

CAR	YEAR MADE	YEAR SOLD	SALE PRICE
Rolls-Royce Silver Ghost	1908	2016	$990,000
Lincoln KB Dual-Cowl Sport Phaeton	1932	2018	$128,800
Volkswagen Beetle	1960	2016	$121,000
Citroën DS23 convertible	1973	2009	$440,000
Plymouth Fury	1958	2015	$198,000
BMC Mini beach car	1961	2014	$181,500
Jaguar E-Type	1963	2017	$7.37 million
Porsche 911 Carrera 2.7 RS	1973	2015	$1.4 million
Ford Mustang Shelby GT500 Super Snake	1967	2019	$2.2 million
Toyota 2000GT	1967	2013	$1.2 million
Dino 246 GTS	1973	2019	$555,000
BMW E9 3.0 CSL	1973	2018	$400,000

INDEX